REVI♡E

100 Inspirational Quotes
for Vital Living

Written by Robert B. Walker

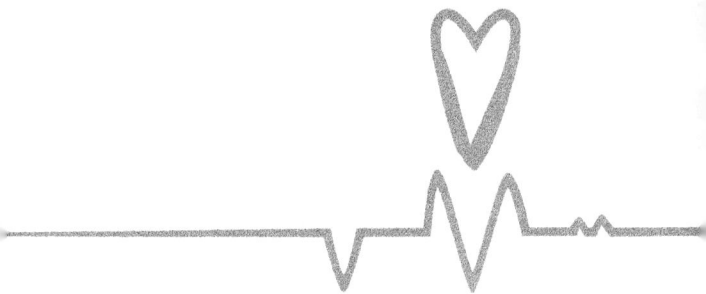

Many times we feel as though our lives are unraveling, or spiraling out of control. Be encouraged. God is just shuffling things around for His purpose. The coming apart is just part of the process God uses to perfect us.

"And I am certain that God, who began the good work within you, will continue his work until it is finally finished on the day when Christ Jesus returns."
Philippians 1:6

Finding relief from the emotional pain of life is tough, but there is a cure: step toward hope. Stepping requires action. Nothing will happen, nor will healing occur, without work. "Toward" is a moving part—moving closer to something, such as a goal or dream. Hope is in the Healer, Jesus, who has you in the palm of His hand, waiting for you to step toward Him.

———⌇M———

"Why am I discouraged?
Why is my heart so sad?
I will put my hope in God!
I will praise him again.
My Savior and my God!"
Psalm 43:5

Pride is the result of trying to steal God's glory for yourself. Instead of self-worship, honor Him with the talent He has given you by sharing His gift to you, with others.

———ᴧᴧ———

"Humble yourselves before the Lord, and he will lift you up in honor."
James 4:10

Decide who you are, what you want to be known for, and how you want to impact the world.

———√⋀———

"Your love for one another will prove to the world
that you are my disciples."
John 13:35

Live in the now, not the yesterday or tomorrow. For the now is where you are. Yesterday is gone, and tomorrow is not here. Let your purpose be about making a difference today.

———∿∿———

"You must warn each other every day, while it is still 'today', so that none of you will be deceived by sin and hardened against God."
Hebrews 3:13

Blessings come from sacrifice.

———⎍⎍———

"Whoever finds their life will lose it, and whoever
loses their life for my sake will find it."
Matthew 10:39

Your talent was given by God. What you achieve with that talent is determined by your drive.

"Commit your actions to the Lord, and your plans will succeed."
Proverbs 16:3

This day is only a small piece of your life journey. As you walk to the land that God has promised you, enjoy this day. It was created for you.

—⎍⋀⎍—

"This is the day the Lord has made. We will rejoice and be glad in it."
Psalm 118:24

Let others see the fire in your eyes to be what you were destined to become.

———⟋⋏⟍———

"You are royal priests, a holy nation, God's very own possession. As a result, you can show others the goodness of God, for he called you out of the darkness into his wonderful light."
1 Peter 2:9

He who blessed you with these gifts and talents will find joy as they are on display for all to see.

—⋎Λ—

"God has given each of you a gift from his great variety of spiritual gifts. Use them well to serve one another."
1 Peter 4:10

The quality of our friendships determines the values of our lives.

"As iron sharpens iron, so a friend sharpens a friend."
Proverbs 27:17

One of the least appreciated skills of successful people is their ability to choose quality friends.

———⋀⋁⋀———

"Don't be fooled by those who say such things, for 'bad company corrupts good character.'"
1 Corinthians 15:33

Be honest, open, and prayerful. Be honest with yourself. Keep an open mind. Pray for God to bless, protect, and guide you.

———ᐯᐯ———

"Be joyful in hope, patient in affliction, faithful in prayer."
Romans 12:12

The difference between good and great is simple: sacrifice. Be up early, stay late, get your rest, then do the rest. It may not always feel the best, but it will be *for* the best.

———⌁———

"So my dear brothers and sisters, be strong and immovable. Always work enthusiastically for the Lord, for you know that nothing you do for the Lord is ever useless."
1 Corinthians 15:58

To be outstanding, choose exceptional people to push you toward your goals.

———ᐯᴧ———

"So encourage each other and build each other up, just as you are already doing."
1 Thessalonians 5:11

If you gave others an all-access pass to your life, what would they find out about you? If there is something you don't want them to see, maybe you need to make a change for a better you.

———⌁———

"Nothing in all creation is hidden from God.
Everything is naked and exposed before his eyes,
and he is the one to whom we are accountable."
Hebrews 4:13

It is never too late to change how people perceive you.

———⎯ᴠᴧ⎯———

"Forget the former things; do not dwell on the past."
Isaiah 43:18

Listen first, be slow to speak, and only give advice when someone asks for it. Many times, people will heal their wounds by having someone with whom to talk. Maybe that is why God created us with two ears and only one tongue.

———⌇———

"Understand this, my dear brothers and sisters: You must all be quick to listen, slow to speak, and slow to get angry."
James 1:19

Our desire for material things in life should not outweigh our appreciation for life.

———⌒⌄⌒———

"Yet true godliness with contentment is itself great wealth. After all, we brought nothing with us when we came into the world, and we can't take anything with us when we leave it. So if we have enough food and clothing, let us be content."
1 Timothy 6:6-8

Find the people who will tell you what you need to hear rather than what you want to hear. These are the people who love you with deep conviction and passion.

——⋀——

"Wounds from a sincere friend are better than
many kisses from an enemy."
Proverbs 27:6

Never let someone walk away wondering if you truly care about them. Say it. Write it. Show it.

"Don't just pretend to love others. Really love them. Hate what is wrong. Hold tightly to what is good. Love each other with genuine affection, and take delight in honoring each other."
Romans 12:9-10

Never be the person who says, "I wish I would have worked harder, studied more, and spoken from my heart." Be the person who lives with passion and endurance.

———⎍⋀⎍———

"Work willingly at whatever you do, as though you were working for the Lord rather than for people."
Colossians 3:23

The sun rises every day. You, too, must rise every day. Rise to the challenges that come with each day.

———⩗⩘———

"Each morning I will sing with joy about your unfailing love."
Psalm 59:16

You will never be on top of the world if you aren't willing to make the climb.

———⩗⩘———

"Being confident of this, that he who began a good work in you will carry it on to completion until the day of Christ Jesus."
Philippians 1:6

You will never win if you aren't willing to lose something.

—–√Λ––—

"If you try to hang on to your life, you will lose it.
But if you give up your life for my sake, you will
save it."
Matthew 16:25

Being driven by a deep desire to be excellent and deeply thankful for the blessings in your life will jumpstart every day.

———⋎⋏⋎———

"The fear of the Lord leads to life; then one rests content, untouched by trouble."
Proverbs 19:23

ACT:
ACCEPT where you are today, but strive for where you want to be tomorrow; COMMIT to getting better, to become better; TRUST God.

———⌁———

"Brothers and sisters, I do not consider myself yet to have taken hold of it. But one thing I do: Forgetting what is behind and straining toward what is ahead, I press on toward the goal to win the prize for which God has called me heavenward in Christ Jesus."
Philippians 3:13-14

There are people who will try to knock you off the path God laid out for you. Find people who will walk God's road with you.

———⟋∿⟍———

"Let us hold unswervingly to the hope we profess, for he who promised is faithful. And let us consider how we may spur one another on toward love and good deeds, not giving up meeting together, as some are in the habit of doing, but encouraging one another..."
Hebrews 10:23-25

A true friendship is born when two people decide that they're willing to be vulnerable.

"We are not withholding our affection from you, but you are withholding yours from us. As a fair exchange – I speak as to my children – open wide your hearts also."
2 Corinthians 6:12-13

Reflect and pause. Reflect on all the good that has happened in your life, and pause to thank the good Lord who made it happen.

"Be thankful in all circumstances, for this is God's will for you who belong to Christ Jesus."
1 Thessalonians 5:18

One of the most beautiful things in life is the calm after the storm.

"He calmed the storm to a whisper and stilled the waves. What a blessing was that stillness as he brought them safely into harbor."
Psalm 107:29-30

**So many people want love, yet so few
are willing to put forth the effort to
develop it. It takes hours of listening and
encouraging others for love to flourish.**

———⎍⋀⎍———

"And so we know and rely on the love God has for
us. God is love. Whoever lives in love lives in God,
and God in them."
1 John 4:16

Pride is like cough syrup, it leaves a bad taste in your mouth. However, after you swallow it, it only has a positive effect.

———√Λ———

"Pride ends in humiliation, while humility brings honor."
Proverbs 29:23

Don't be satisfied with mediocrity. Find a way to excel.

"Since you excel in so many ways – in your faith, your gifted speakers, your knowledge, your enthusiasm, and your love from us – I want you to excel also in this gracious act of giving."
2 Corinthians 8:7

If who you are is not who you want to be, stop making excuses, and start making an effort to become that person.

"For we are God's handiwork, created in Christ Jesus to do good works, which God prepared in advance for us to do."
Ephesians 2:10

Invest your time with people who will cultivate growth in your life.

—⎍◊⎍—

"Let the message of Christ dwell among you richly
as you teach and admonish one another with all
wisdom through psalms, hymns, and songs from
the Spirit..."
Colossians 3:16

The building blocks of success are the things you do not like to do. However, these will form a foundation that allows you to do what you want to do.

"Commit to the Lord whatever you do, and he will establish your plans."
Proverbs 16:3

Build bridges to people. This will allow you to construct relationships that have lasting value in your life.

———⌇———

"Do not let any unwholesome talk come out of your mouths, but only what is helpful for building others up according to their needs, that it may benefit those who listen."
Ephesians 4:29

The fear of rejection will paralyze your soul.

"For God has not given us a spirit of fear and timidity, but of power, love, and self-discipline."
2 Timothy 1:7

You can borrow a suit, lease a car and rent a house. But you must own your character, and it will be defined by who you are and what you do.

———⩗———

"Since God chose you to be the holy people he loves, you must clothe yourselves with tenderhearted mercy, kindness, humility, gentleness, and patience."
Colossians 3:12

You cannot micromanage God.

"For the life of every living thing is in his hand, and
the breath of every human being."
Job 12:10

The people who go with you today may not be the people who need to go with you tomorrow. If they cannot grow with you, they should not go with you.

———⌇———

"The godly give good advice to their friends; the wicked lead them astray."
Proverbs 12:26

In five years, if you find yourself still hanging around the same crowd, going to the same places, and speaking the same way, you may not be growing. The people you are with may be holding you back from your true potential.

———ⱴᴧ———

"This means that anyone who belongs to Christ has become a new person. The old life is gone; a new life has begun!"
2 Corinthians 5:17

Live everyday prepared to say goodbye because one day you will.

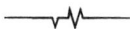

—⎍◠⎍—

"For everything there is a season, a time for every
activity under heaven."
Ecclesiastes 3:1

Do not let where you come from keep you from getting where you want to go.

———⎍⋀⎍———

"No, dear brothers and sisters, I have not achieved it, but I focus on this one thing: Forgetting the past and looking forward to what lies ahead, I press on to reach the heavenly prize for which God, through Christ Jesus, is calling us."
Philippians 3:13-14

What can you give a person who has everything? Words of affirmation, love, and encouragement. No amount of money can buy this.

———√W———

"Kind words are like honey- sweet to the soul and
healthy for the body."
Proverbs 16:24

Prepare to be the best physically, mentally, emotionally, and spiritually. No earthquake can topple these pillars of success.

——⌄⋀——

"Because we have these promises, dear friends, let us cleanse ourselves from everything that can defile our body or spirit. And let us work toward complete holiness because we fear God."
2 Corinthians 7:1

Quality people attract quality people.

———⩗⩘———

"A good tree can't produce bad fruit, and a bad tree
can't produce good fruit."
Matthew 7:18

Leadership can be very lonely and frustrating. Sometimes the decisions you make will hurt others, but you were chosen to lead. Lead by being prayerful and discerning.

———✓∿———

"Devote yourselves to prayer with an alert mind
and a thankful heart."
Colossians 4:2

Wherever you are in ten years is exactly where you are supposed to be. Embrace God's plan and not your own.

—⎺⋀⎽—

"You can make plans, but the Lord's purpose will prevail."
Proverbs 12:26

A happy person is one who believes he is too blessed to be stressed.

———√∿———

"Give your burdens to the Lord, and he will take
care of you. He will not permit the godly to slip and
fall."
Psalm 55:22

True love comes from being true to our values, morals, and God.

"Love is patient, love is kind. It does not envy, it does not boast, it is not proud. It does not dishonor others, it is not self-seeking, it is not easily angered, it keeps no record of wrongs. Love does not delight in evil but rejoices with the truth."
1 Corinthians 13:4-6

**This world is only hopeless when we
refuse to be the hope for others.**

"We who are strong ought to bear with the fails of
the weak and not to please ourselves. Each of us
should please our neighbors for their good, to build
them up."
Romans 15:1-2

There is a constant battle between freedom and control, but you cannot gain freedom without self-control.

———⩘———

"Like a city whose walls are broken through
is a person who lacks self-control."
Proverbs 25:28

Live life with purpose and passion. Death is coming for all of us, so leave a legacy and enjoy God's goodness.

———✓⋀———

"But I have raised you up for this very purpose, that I might show you my power and that my name might be proclaimed in all the earth."
Exodus 9:16

There will be times your body and mind want to give up, but you can never let your heart give up. Even broken hearts keep beating.

———⩗—

"Therefore, since through God's mercy we have this ministry, we do not lose heart."
2 Corinthians 4:13

Laugh like a five-year-old. Run like you are twelve. Love with the passion of a twenty-year-old. Think with the wisdom of an eighty-year-old.

"Teach us to remember our days, that we may gain a heart of wisdom."
Psalm 90:12

Be the hope so that others may find their own.

———⎺⋀⋁⋀⎽———

"May the God of hope fill you with all joy and peace
as you trust in Him, so that you may overflow with
the hope by the power of the Holy Spirit."
Romans 15:13

Build up those who will continue your legacy.

"And the things that you have heard from me among many witnesses, commit these to faithful men who will be able to teach others also."
2 Timothy 2:2

**God puts setbacks in our lives to see if
we have the heart for a comeback.**

———⌄⋀⌄———

"Blessed is the one who perseveres under trial
because, having stood the test, that person will
receive the crown of life that the Lord has promised
to those who love him."
James 1:12

Some people say, "I love you" with words but never with deeds. True love is a combination of the two.

"Dear children, let us not love with words or speech but with actions and in truth."
1 John 3:18

Learn how to appreciate the sacrifices that people make for you.

—⎯ᴧ⎯—

"There is no greater love than to lay down one's life for one's friends."
John 15:13

Most people define success by what they personally earn or gain. True success is defined by impacting people's lives for the better.

"Be kind and compassionate to one another, forgiving each other, just as in Christ God forgave you."
Ephesians 4:32

Just because the eternal battle has been won doesn't mean you should quit fighting.

"You armed me with strength for battle; you humbled my adversaries before me."
Psalm 18:39

It is very difficult to bear new fruit in old soil. Sometimes, it is best to start over.

"Therefore, if anyone is in Christ, the new creation has come: The old has gone and the new is here!"
2 Corinthians 5:17

If the glass looks half empty, pour it in a smaller glass.

———⎺⋀⎽———

"They count on it but are disappointed. When they
arrive, their hopes are dashed."
Job 6:20

Be a giver of encouragement, and watch how encouragement will find its way back to you.

———ᴠᴧ———

"Let everything you say be good and helpful, so that your words will be an encouragement to those who hear them."
Ephesians 4:29

Don't let others tell you how to think. Find a way to make others think.

"I meditate on your precepts and consider your ways."
Psalm 119: 15

Never compromise words you spoke to God, and never compromise words God spoke to you.

———ᴧᴧ———

"If anyone, then, knows the good they ought to do
and doesn't do it, it is sin for them."
James 4:17

**Comparing yourself to others limits what
you can achieve.**

———⌇⌇———

"Pay careful attention to your own work, for then
you will get the satisfaction of a job well done, and
you won't need to compare yourself to anyone
else."
Galatians 6:4

Those who embrace availability will be present for the success that comes their way.

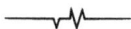

———∿———

"Then I heard the Lord asking, 'Whom should I send as a messenger to this people? Who will go for us?' I said, 'Here I am. Send me.'"
Isaiah 6:8

Smiling is the easiest way to share the joy in your heart.

———⌇⋏⋏—————

"A glad heart makes a happy face; a broken heart
crushed the spirit."
Proverbs 15:13

You need to remember the bad times in your life to appreciate the good times.

———ᴧᴧ———

"Weeping may last through the night, but joy comes
with the morning."
Psalm 30:5

**People are attracted to things that shine.
Be the light and shine for all to see.**

———∿∿———

"You are the light of the world – like a city on a
hilltop that cannot be hidden. No one lights a
lamp then puts it under a basket. Instead, a lamp is
placed on a stand, where it gives light to everyone
in the house. In the same way, let your good deeds
shine out for all to see, so that everyone will praise
your heavenly Father."
Matthew 5:14-16

Be with those who are running after God at the same pace you are; don't slow your pace down for others. If they want to run the race of life with you, they can work to catch up.

———∿———

"Don't you realize that in a race everyone runs, but only one person gets the prize? So run to win!"
1 Corinthians 9:24

**You can't change people, and you may
not be able to change the world. However,
you can change the people you let into
your world and how you impact them.**

———⌇\/\———

"Walk with the wise and become wise; associate
with fools and get in trouble."
Proverbs 13:20

The biggest myth in leadership is that you control other people. In reality, the people you lead actually have more influence on you by the way they perform.

———⟋◟⟍———

"Instruct the wise and they will be wiser still;
teach the righteous and they will add to their
learning."
Proverbs 9:9

Blue skies always lie behind clouds.

———╴╱╲╴———

"I have placed my rainbow in the clouds. It is a sign
of my covenant with you and with all the earth."
Genesis 9:13

Life is best when you can find someone with whom to laugh.

———√Λ———

"So I commend the enjoyment of life, because there is nothing better for a person under the sun than to eat and drink and be glad. Then joy will accompany them in their toil all the days of the life God has given them under the sun."
Ecclesiastes 8:15

No one plants seeds without a plan to harvest.

———⩗Μ———

"A man reaps what he sows."
Galatians 6:7

Don't let your love for this world be greater than your love for the Lord.

———⌇———

"Do not love the world or anything in the world. If anyone loves the world, love for the Father is not in them...The world and its desires pass away, but whoever does the will of God lives forever."
John 12:15, 17

True peace is when you embrace your gifts with His confidence, not your own.

"There are different kinds of gifts, but the same spirit distributes them. There are different kinds of service, but the same Lord. There are different kinds of working, but in all of them and in everyone it is the same God at work."
1 Corinthians 12:4-6

A willing heart is a good start.

"If you are willing and obedient, you will eat the
good things of the land."
Isaiah 1:19

Love will propel you; hate will destroy you.

———⋎⋀⋎———

"Hatred stirs up conflict, but love covers over all
wrongs."
Proverbs 10:12

Walking in the dark with someone else is no better than walking alone, unless you are both heading toward the light. Be the one to lead others out of darkness.

"For you were once darkness, but now you are light in the Lord. Live as children of light."
Ephesians 5:8

Know yourself before you request others to.

———√Λ———

"Do not think of yourself more highly than you ought, but rather think of yourself with sober judgement, in accordance with the faith God has distributed to each of you."
Romans 12:3

Eternity will come when tomorrow does not.

———⌁———

"Look! I am creating new heavens and a new earth,
and no one will even think about the old ones
anymore."
Isaiah 65:17

Just because you are going places doesn't mean you are heading in the right direction. Determine where you want to go before you begin.

———⌁⌁———

"Show me the right path, O Lord; point out the road
for me to follow."
Psalm 25:4

We always think to pay back others who have invested money in us, but we rarely think to pay back those who invested their love in us.

"If you are good to these people and do your best to please them and give them a favorable answer, they will always be your loyal subjects."
2 Chronicles 10:7

Praise God for the storms of life. Growth cannot come without a little rain.

———⌇———

"Consider it pure joy, my brothers and sisters, whenever you face trials of many kinds, because you know that the testing of your faith produces perseverance."
James 1:2-3

The Son shines even when the sun does not.

———⌇———

"When Jesus spoke again to the people, he said, 'I
am the light of the world. Whoever follows me will
never walk in darkness, but will have the light of
life.'"
John 8:12

Life is full of curves, but it always straightens out.

"The valleys will be filled, and the mountains and hills made level. The curves will be straightened, and the rough places made smooth."
Luke 3:5

Don't waste your time worrying about the fight; the battle has already been won.

———∿∿———

"This is what the Lord says to you: 'Do not be afraid
or discouraged because of this vast army. For the
battle is not yours, but God's.'"
2 Chronicles 20:15

**Being a leader means being vulnerable.
You have to put yourself on the front lines
and risk it all for what you believe in.**

———~\/\~———

"Whoever wants to become great among you must
be your servant, and whoever wants to be first
must be your slave, just as the Son of Man did not
come to be served, but to serve..."
Matthew 20:26-28

Your bed can be a place of rest or a place keeping you from success.

———⩗⩘———

"A wise youth harvests in the summer, but one who
sleeps during harvest is a disgrace."
Proverbs 10:5

Life should be about substance, not stuff.

———⎯⋀⎯———

"Whoever loves money never has enough; whoever
loves wealth is never satisfied with their income.
This too is meaningless."
Ecclesiastes 5:10

Do not allow your mind to have control over your heart.

"Above all else, guard your heart, for everything you
do flows from it."
Proverbs 4:23

**There are those who *talk* about doing,
and there are those who *do*.**

"I can do all things through Christ who strengthens
me."
Philippians 4:13

The seemingly insignificant choices you make every day are determining whether or not you are fulfilling your destiny.

"Trust in the lord with all your heart; do not depend on your own understanding. Seek his will in all you do, and he will show you which path to take."
Proverbs 3:5-6

Don't turn from God's plan just because it doesn't align with your own.

———⎯⌁⎯———

"The Lord says, 'I will guide you along the best pathway for your life. I will advise you and watch over you.'"
Psalm 32:8

REVIVE

Acknowledgments

I want to acknowledge and say thank you to all those that helped with this project:

Drew Hardee
Izabella Miranda
Elizabeth McNeil
Renata Bolden
Lindsay Adams
Janice White
Crystal Rhodes
Kevin Horner
Sharon Wade
Minnie Miller
Sarah Layne
Savanna Coleman
Krystil Irvin
Stephen Copeland

A very special thank you to Sarah Jackson Cullen and Nadia Michelle Guy for helping to complete *Revive*. Your diligence and commitment made *Revive* a reality for so many. Thank you Sarah and Nadia for your sacrifices.

Additional Books by
Robert B. Walker

To order the books below,
visit www.thecoremediagroup.com

ADvantage: The Athletic Director's Ultimate Resource™

All the rules, regulations, policies, procedures, and forms and Athletic Director needs to operate an efficient and effective athletic program in a single source, and everyone can be customized! No more wasted time searching for the right form or procedures document. It's all right here, a wealth of information in one volume, and easily downloaded in a Microsoft Word format for you. Customize and duplicate as much as you need.

Drive Thru Success

What if finding success was as simple as ordering a combo at your favorite fast-food chain? In *Drive Thru Success*, author Robert B. Walker takes a refreshingly simple look at life as it relates to the drive thru experience. Chapter after chapter, Walker's positive-thinking approach to the ups and downs of life will leave you ready to make the most of your own lives, and perhaps a little hungry too.

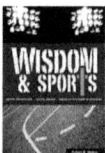

Wisdom & Sports

In *Wisdom & Sports*, verses from all 31 chapters of Proverbs are paired with spiritually encouraging stories of well-known athletes and thought-provoking devotionals. You will be inspired as you read each page of this book written by Robert B. Walker.

Living the Thankful Life

Living the Thankful Life includes 29 short stories about things for which Robert B. Walker is thankful. It also includes an area to write your own stories of thanks, which enables you to make it a legacy book for you, your family and others concerning living a thankful life.

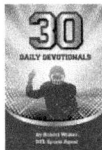

30 Daily Football Devotionals

30 Daily Football Devotionals contains 30 daily readings related to football. Each day contains a bible verse and an inspirational story or thought to encourage you on and off the field. Included are areas for you to write notes or personal stories that you can reflect upon throughout your athletic career.

Revive: 100 Athletic Quotes for Your Athlete

Revive: 100 Quotes for the Athlete is the second book to be released in the *Revive* series. It features 100 quotes for athletes on personal growth and sportsmanship. This book is a great resource for daily encouragement and will help you progress in your athletic life.

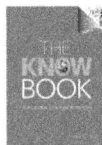

The Know Book/The Know Journal

What do you know? This life is filled with patterns-some obvious, some hidden. Whether we realize it or not, as we experience life-encountering situations, building relationships, making connections-we learn more and more about these rhythms of human existence. The question isn't whether or not these patterns exist. The important question to ask yourself is, "How much do I know?" Through fifty-two easily digestible chapters, *The Know Book* breaks down these themes of life and provides a guide for navigating through them. You've had the experiences, the relationships, and the personal convictions. Here's your chance to rediscover what you've known all along.

www.ingramcontent.com/pod-product-compliance
Lightning Source LLC
Chambersburg PA
CBHW071010040426
42443CB00007B/745